PRAYER: BEHOLDING GOD'S GLORY

by an unknown Christian

D1571062

NAVPRESS ◖

A MINISTRY OF THE NAVIGATORS
P.O. BOX 6000, COLORADO SPRINGS, COLORADO 80934

The Navigators is an international Christian organization. Our mission is to reach, disciple, and equip people to know Christ and to make Him known through successive generations. We envision multitudes of diverse people in the United States and every other nation who have a passionate love for Christ, live a lifestyle of sharing Christ's love, and multiply spiritual laborers among those without Christ.

NavPress is the publishing ministry of The Navigators. NavPress publications help believers learn biblical truth and apply what they learn to their lives and ministries. Our mission is to stimulate spiritual formation among our readers.

The content of this booklet is adapted from _THE KNEELING CHRISTIAN_ by An Unknown Christian. Copyright 1971 by Zondervan Publishing House. Used by permission. To fully benefit from the message, the reader is encouraged to enjoy a complete reading of _The Kneeling Christian_, which is available through Christian bookstores.

Unless otherwise identified, all Scripture quotations in this publication are from the _Holy Bible: New International Version_ (NIV), Copyright © 1973, 1978, 1984, International Bible Society. Used by permission of Zondervan Bible Publishers. Another version used is the _King James Version_ (KJV).

Printed in the United States of America

4 5 6 7 8 9 10 11 12 13 14 15 16 17 / 99 98 97

FOR A FREE CATALOG OF
NAVPRESS BOOKS & BIBLE STUDIES,
CALL 1-800-366-7788 (USA)
or 1-416-499-4615 (CANADA)

PRAYER: BEHOLDING GOD'S GLORY

What Is Prayer?

What do we mean by prayer? I believe the vast majority of Christians would say, "Prayer is asking things from God." But surely prayer is much more than merely getting God to run our errands for us.

The word *prayer* really means "a wish directed toward," that is, toward God. All that true prayer seeks is God Himself, for with Him we get all we need. Prayer is simply "the turning of the soul to God." David described it as the lifting up of the soul to God. "To you, O LORD, I lift up my soul" (Psalm 25:1). What a description that is! When we lift up our souls to God in prayer, it gives God an opportunity to do what He will in us and with us. It is putting ourselves at God's disposal. God is always on our side, but we are not always on His side. When man prays, it is God's opportunity.

"Prayer," said an old Jewish mystic, "is

the moment when Heaven and earth kiss each other."

Prayer, then, is certainly not persuading God to do what we want Him to do. It is not bending the will of a reluctant God to our will. It does not change His purpose, although it may release His power. "We must not conceive of prayer as overcoming God's reluctance," said Archbishop Trench, "but as laying hold of His highest willingness."

For God always purposes our greatest good. Even the prayer offered in ignorance and blindness cannot swerve Him from that, although, when we persistently pray for some harmful thing, our willfulness may bring it about, and we suffer accordingly. "He gave them their request," said the psalmist; "but sent leanness into their soul" (Psalm 106:15, KJV). They brought this "leanness" upon themselves. They were "cursed with the burden of a granted prayer."

Some people think prayer is only for emergencies! Danger threatens, sickness comes, things are lacking, difficulties arise—then they pray like the atheist down a coal mine: when the roof began to fall he began to pray.

Prayer, however, is much more than merely asking God for something—although that is a very valuable part of prayer (if only because it reminds us of our utter dependence upon God). It is also communion with God, talking with (not only to) God. We get to know

4

people by talking with them. We get to know God in like manner. The highest result of prayer is not deliverance from evil, or the securing of some coveted thing, but knowledge of God. "Now this is eternal life: that they may know you, the only true God" (John 17:3). Yes, prayer discovers more of God, and that is the soul's greatest discovery. People still cry out, "If only I knew where to find him; if only I could go to his dwelling" (Job 23:3)!

A Vision of God

The kneeling Christian always finds God, and is found by Him. The vision of the Lord Jesus blinded Saul of Tarsus, but he tells us that later when he was praying in the Temple at Jerusalem he fell into a trance and saw Jesus (Acts 22:18). Then Christ commissioned Saul to go to the Gentiles. Vision is always a precursor of vocation and venture. It was so with Isaiah. "I saw the Lord seated on a throne, high and exalted" (Isaiah 6:1). This vision also was a prelude to a call to service: "Go" (verse 9). Now, we cannot get a vision of God unless we pray. And where there is no vision the soul perishes (Proverbs 29:18).

A vision of God! Brother Lawrence said, "Prayer is nothing else than a sense of God's presence"—what more do we desire? Was the psalmist of old conscious of such a thought when he cried, "Find rest, O my soul, in God alone" (Psalm 62:5)?

5

I believe that much of our failure in prayer is due to the fact that we have not looked into this question, "What is prayer?" It is good to be conscious that we are always in the presence of God. It is better to gaze upon Him in adoration. But it is best of all to commune with Him as a friend—and that is prayer.

Real prayer reveals a soul athirst for God—for God alone. Real prayer comes from the lips of those whose affection is set on things above. What a man of prayer Zinzendorf was. Why? He sought the Giver rather than His gifts. He said, "I have one passion: it is He, He alone." Even the Muslim sees that there are three degrees in prayer. The lowest is that spoken only by the lips. The second is when, by a resolute effort, we succeed in fixing our thoughts on divine things. The third is when the soul finds it hard to turn away from God.

Of course, we know that God bids us *ask* of Him. We may rest assured that prayer both pleases God and supplies all our need. A strange child he is who only seeks his father's presence when he desires a gift from him! Don't we yearn to rise to a higher level of prayer than mere petition? How is it to be done?

Beholding God's Glory and Grace

It seems to me that only two steps are necessary—or shall I say two thoughts? There must be, first of all, a realization of God's glory, and then of God's grace. We sometimes sing:

Grace and glory flow from Thee;
Shower, O shower them, Lord, on me.

Nor is such a desire fanciful, although some may ask what God's glory has to do with prayer.

But ought we not to remind ourselves who He is to whom we pray? There is logic in the couplet:

Thou art coming to a King;
Large petitions with thee bring.

Do you think any of us spends enough time marveling over God's exceeding great glory? Do you suppose any of us has grasped the full meaning of the word *grace*? Are not our prayers so often ineffective and powerless because we rush unthinkingly and unpreparedly into God's presence? We pray without realizing the majesty and glory of the God whom we are approaching and without reflecting upon the exceeding great riches of His glory in Christ Jesus, which we hope to draw upon. We must "think magnificently of God."

May I then suggest that before we lay our petitions before God we first dwell on His glory and then on His grace—for He offers us both. We must lift up the soul to God. Let us place ourselves, as it were, in the presence of God and direct our prayer to "the King of kings and Lord of lords, who alone is immortal and who lives in unapproachable light" (1 Timothy

6:15-16). Let us then give Him adoration and praise because of His exceeding great glory. Consecration is not enough. There must be adoration.

"Holy, holy, holy is the LORD Almighty," cry the seraphim; "the whole earth is full of his glory" (Isaiah 6:3). "Glory to God in the highest," cries the heavenly host (Luke 2:14). Yet some of us try to commune with God without stopping to take off our shoes on holy ground (Exodus 3:5).

But we may approach His glory with boldness. Did not our Lord pray that His disciples might behold His glory (John 17:24)? Why? It was not a desire for self-display that led Jesus to pray, "Father, glorify me" (John 17:5). Our Lord wants us to realize His infinite trustworthiness and unlimited power, so that we can approach Him in simple faith and trust.

So we must get a glimpse of that glory before we can pray aright. Therefore our Lord said, "This, then, is how you should pray: 'Our Father in heaven [the realm of glory], hallowed be your name'" (Matthew 6:9). There is nothing like a glimpse of glory to banish fear and doubt.

Before we offer our petitions, may it not help us to offer our adoration in the words of praise used by some of the saints of old? Some devout souls may not need such help. We are told that Francis of Assisi would frequently spend an hour or two in prayer on Mount Averno, while the only word that escaped his

8

lips would be "God" repeated at intervals. He began with adoration—and often stopped there!

But most of us need some help to realize the glory of the invisible God before we can adequately adore Him. William Law said, "When you begin to pray, use such expressions of the attributes of God as will make you sensible of His greatness and power."

Some of us begin every day with a glance heavenward while saying, "Glory be to the Father, and to the Son, and to the Holy Spirit." The prayer "O Lord God most holy, O Lord most mighty, O holy and merciful Savior!" is often enough to bring a solemn awe and a spirit of holy adoration upon the soul. A verse of a hymn may serve the same purpose.

My God, how wonderful Thou art!
    Thy majesty how bright.
How beautiful Thy mercy-seat
    In depths of burning light!
How wonderful, how beautiful
    The sight of Thee must be;
Thine endless wisdom, boundless power
    And awful purity.

This is what carries us into the very heavenlies!

We need to cry out, and cry often, "My soul glorifies the Lord and my spirit rejoices in God my Savior" (Luke 1:46-47). Can we catch the spirit of the psalmist and sing, "Praise the LORD, O my soul. O LORD my God, you are very great; you are clothed with splendor and majesty" (Psalm 104:1). When shall we learn that "in his temple all cry, 'Glory!'" (Psalm 29:9)? Let us, too, cry, "Glory!"

Preparing for Glory in Us

Such worship of God not only puts us into the spirit of prayer, but in some mysterious way it helps God to work on our behalf. Do you remember those wonderful words, "He who sacrifices thank offerings honors me, and he prepares the way so that I may show him the salvation of God" (Psalm 50:23)? Praise and thanksgiving not only open the gates of Heaven for me to approach God, but also "prepare the way" for God to bless me. The Apostle Paul cried, "Rejoice evermore" before he said, "Pray without ceasing" (1 Thessalonians 5:16-17, KJV). So then our praise, as well as our prayers, is to be without ceasing.

"For from him and through him and to him are all things. To him be the glory forever!" (Romans 11:36). This is the God who bids us come to Him in prayer. This God is our God, and He has gifts for us. God says that everyone called by His name has been created for His glory (Isaiah 43:7). His Church is to be a glorious Church—holy and without blemish (Ephesians 5:27). Have you ever fully realized that the Lord Jesus desires to share with us the glory we see in Him? This is His great gift to you and me, His redeemed ones. Believe me,

10

the more we have of God's glory, the less we will seek His gifts.

Not only "on the day he comes to be glorified in his holy people" (2 Thessalonians 1:10) is there glory for us, but here and now—today. He wishes us to be partakers of His glory. "I have given them the glory you gave me," Jesus declares (John 17:22). What is God's command? "Arise, shine, for your light has come, and the glory of the LORD rises upon you" (Isaiah 60:1).

God would have people say of us as Peter said of the disciples of old, "The Spirit of glory and of God rests on you" (1 Peter 4:14). Would not that be an answer to most of our prayers? Could we ask for anything better? How can we get this glory? How are we to reflect it? Only as the result of prayer. It is when we pray that the Holy Spirit takes of the things of Christ and reveals them to us.

When Moses prayed, "Show me your glory," he not only saw but shared something of that glory, and his own face shone with the light of it (Exodus 33:18, 34:29). And when we, too, gaze on "the glory of God in the face of Christ" (2 Corinthians 4:6), we see not only a glimpse of that glory, but we gain something of it ourselves.

Now, that is prayer, and the highest result of prayer. Nor is there any other way of securing that glory, that God may be glorified in us.

Our Lord's first disciples said in awed

tones, "We beheld his glory!" What followed? A few obscure fishermen companied with Christ a little while, seeing His glory, and lo, they themselves caught something of it! Then others marveled and "took note that these men had been with Jesus" (Acts 4:13). And when we can declare, "Our fellowship is with the Father and with his Son, Jesus Christ" (1 John 1:3), people will say the same of us: "They have been with Jesus!"

"The secret of failure is that we see men rather than God." Is it not time that we got a new vision of God in all His glory? Who can say what will happen when the Church sees God? But let us not wait for others. Let us, each one for himself, with unveiled face and unsullied heart, get this vision of the glory of the Lord. "Blessed are the pure in heart, for they will see God" (Matthew 5:8).

Must We Agonize?

Perhaps my words remind you of people who spend all day or night on their knees before God, refusing food and scorning sleep while they pray and pray and pray. You may be anxiously wondering, "Am I expected to pray like that?"

Child of God, do not let such fears distress you. Prayer is measured, not by time, but by intensity. Just be willing to do what God will have you do—what He leads you to do. Think about it; pray about it. We pray to a loving heavenly Father. We sometimes sing, "Oh, how He loves!" And nothing can fathom that love.

Prayer is not given as a burden to be borne, or an irksome duty to fulfill, but as an unlimited joy and power. It is given that we may "find grace to help us in our time of need" (Hebrews 4:16), and every time is a time of need. "Pray" is an invitation to be accepted rather than a command to be obeyed. Is it a burden for a child to come to his father to ask for some benefit? How a father loves his child, and seeks his highest good! How he shields that little one from any sorrow or suffering! Our heavenly Father loves us infinitely more than any earthly father. "Your heavenly father knows," says our Lord (Matthew 6:32); and if He knows, we can trust and not be afraid.

A schoolmaster may blame a boy for neglected homework or for unpunctual attendance, but the loving father in the home knows all about it. He knows about the boy's devoted service at home, where sickness or poverty throws so many tasks in his way. Our Father sees. He knows how little leisure some of us have for prolonged periods of prayer.

For some of us God makes leisure. He makes us lie down that He may make us look up. Even then, weakness of body often prevents prolonged prayer. Yet I question if any of us, however great and reasonable our excuses, spend enough thought over our prayers.

Some of us are bound to be much in

prayer. Our very work demands it. We may be looked upon as spiritual leaders; we may have the spiritual welfare or training of others. God forbid that we should sin against the Lord in ceasing to pray enough for them (1 Samuel 12:23). Others carry beloved unbelievers in their hearts, for whom they cannot help praying.

But how well we know the difficulties that surround the prayer life of many! Busy mothers and homemakers who scarcely know how to get through the endless washing and cooking, mending and cleaning, shopping and visiting. Or tired workers who are too weary to pray when the day's work is done.

Child of God, our heavenly Father knows all about it. He is not a taskmaster. He is our Father. If you have no time for prayer, or no chance of secret prayer, just tell Him about it—and you will discover you are praying!

Can we make time for prayer? I may be wrong, but my own belief is that it is not God's will for most of us—and perhaps not for any of us—to spend so much time in prayer as to injure our physical health through getting insufficient food or sleep. With many it is a physical impossibility, because of bodily weakness, to remain long in the spirit of intense prayer.

The inspired command is clear enough: We "should always pray and not give up" (Luke 18:1). This cannot mean we are to be always on our knees. God does not wish us to

14

neglect rightful work in order to pray. But it is equally certain that we might work better and do more work if we gave less time to work and more to prayer.

Let us work well. "If a man will not work, he shall not eat" (2 Thessalonians 3:10). But are there not endless opportunities every day of lifting up holy hearts in prayer to our Father? Do we seize the opportunity, as we open our eyes each new day, of praising our Redeemer? We can pray as we dress. Without a reminder we will often forget, so stick a note, "Pray without ceasing," to your mirror. We can pray as we go from one duty to another. We can often pray at our work. The washing and writing, mending and minding, cooking and cleaning will be done all the better for it.

"Do not be anxious about anything, but in everything, by prayer and petition, with thanksgiving, present your requests to God" (Philippians 4:6). Does not "in everything" suggest that, as thing after thing befalls us, moment by moment, we should then and there make it a thing of prayer and praise to the Lord who is near? Prayer is to a near-God. When our Lord sent His disciples forth to work, He said, "Surely I am with you always" (Matthew 28:20).

But I question if this habitual communion with our blessed Lord is possible unless we have times—whether long or brief—of definite prayer. Now, the devil opposes our approach to God in prayer, and does all he can to prevent the prayer of faith. His chief way of hindering us is to try to fill our minds with the thought of our needs, so that they will not be occupied with thoughts of our loving Father, to whom we pray. The devil wants us to think more of the gift than of the Giver. The Holy Spirit leads us to pray for a brother. We get as far as "O God, bless my brother"—and away go our thoughts to the brother, and his difficulties, his hopes and his fears, and away goes prayer!

How hard the devil makes it for us to concentrate on God! This is why we urge people to get a realization of the glory of God, and His power and presence, before offering up any petition.

What is prayer? It is a sign of spiritual life. I should as soon expect life in a dead man as spiritual life in a prayerless soul! Our spirituality and our fruitfulness are always in proportion to the reality of our prayers. If, then, we have at all wandered away from home in the matter of prayer, let us today resolve, "I will set out and go back to my father and say to him: Father . . ." (Luke 15:18).

Summary

True prayer is a turning of the soul to God with a thirst to know Him. Its fruits are a vision of God and of our unique calling. True prayer begins when we place ourselves in God's presence to behold His glory and grace, and adore Him. Praise prepares the way for God to bless us, to impart His own glory to us so that the world can see it.

Prayer is measured not by time but by intensity. Our Father understands the pressures on our lives, and He invites us to pray to Him in all our daily circumstances. Still, this constant practice of God's presence is probably impossible unless we set aside some time each day just for prayer. The devil will do anything he can to prevent this, but we can defeat him if we determine to focus on God's glory.

For Reflection and Action

1. a. Read Psalm 63:1. To what extent are you as thirsty for God as David was?

   b. The Bible suggests that it's as normal for humans to thirst for God as for water. If

17

you are thirsty for Him, why are you? If not, what do you think is preventing you from feeling that normal thirst?

2. Do you find it easy to spend time praising God? Why or why not?

3. What inner attitudes and outer circumstances most hinder you from spending time in God's presence adoring Him?

4. a. What can you do to reduce these obstacles?

b. What can you ask God to do?

5. Take ten minutes to adore God for His glory
   and grace. Find a place where you can be
   alone. If you need help concentrating on
   Him for this amount of time, read some or
   all of Psalm 62-66, 103-104. Then, write
   your praises on a piece of paper. Both reading aloud and writing will help you keep
   from being distracted.

For Meditation

If you memorize psalms or parts of psalms, you
can pray them back to God when you are driv-
ing or working. You can use them as spring-
boards to launch you into adoring God in your
own words.

Copy part or all of the following passage
onto a card and tape it where you will see it
several times a day (over your desk, on your
refrigerator, on your bathroom mirror). Each
day, read at least one verse aloud seven times,
or until you have memorized it. At other times
during the day, think about what the truths
about God in that verse mean to you. When
you've digested one verse, go on to the next.

Praise the LORD, O my soul;
* all my inmost being, praise his holy*
* name.*

Praise the LORD, O my soul,
*   and forget not all his benefits—*
who forgives all your sins
*   and heals all your diseases,*
who redeems your life from the pit
*   and crowns you with love and*
*   compassion,*
who satisfies your desires with good
*   things*
*   so that your youth is renewed like*
*   the eagle's. . . .*

The LORD is compassionate and
*   gracious,*
*   slow to anger, abounding in love.*
He will not always accuse,
*   nor will he harbor his anger forever;*
he does not treat us as our sins deserve
*   or repay us according to our*
*   iniquities.*
For as high as the heavens are above the
*   earth,*
*   so great is his love for those who*
*   fear him. (Psalm 103:1-5,8-11)*

The NavPress Booklet Series includes:

A Woman of Excellence
  by Cynthia Heald

Avoiding Common Financial Mistakes
  by Ron Blue

Building Your Child's Self-Esteem
  by Gary Smalley & John Trent

Claiming the Promise
  by Doug Sparks

Dealing with Desires You Can't Control
  by Mark R. McMinn

God Cares About Your Work
  by Doug Sherman & William Hendricks

How to Deal with Anger
  by Larry Crabb

How to Handle Stress
  by Don Warrick

How to Have a Quiet Time
  by Warren & Ruth Myers

**How to Keep Your Head Up
When Your Job's Got You Down**
  by Doug Sherman

How to Know God's Will
  by Charles Stanley

How to Overcome Loneliness
  by Elisabeth Elliot

Prayer: Beholding God's Glory

When You Disagree: Resolving Marital Conflicts
  by Jack & Carole Mayhall

You Can Trust God
  by Jerry Bridges